Rugby Union

Training and Education Associates Ltd.
41 Paradise Walk, London SW3 4JW
Telephone 01-351 1151

A division of the Talking Pictures Group

Published-1974
Published in paperback-1973
© Training and Education Associates Ltd. 1974
World Copyright reserved
ISBN 85961 031 4

Acknowledgments for editorial, technical, and photographic
assistance:
Don Rutherford, Director of Coaching
Peter Brook
Don Davis

Printed in England for National Westminster Bank Ltd.   TEAL 12

Foreword

Increased leisure time is encouraging more people to participate in sport, creating a need for more coaching material.

This series of booklets provides a valuable introduction to learning the skills of many popular sports and forms a part of the audio-visual programmes. The filmstrips and booklets have been prepared in co-operation with the national coaches for each sport.

All coaches and others concerned in introducing sport, especially to newcomers, will welcome this series and commend the producers and the National Westminster Bank, who have given their support to this worthwhile project.

Peter Lawson

P. Lawson
General Secretary

Central Council of Physical Recreation

Introduction

The game of Rugby football dates back to the year 1823, with its origins in England, although it is now controlled by the International Rugby Football Board.

Rugby football is very much an international game, but it also has a very strong following in the armed services, county clubs, Universities and schools. It is a game that is enjoyed from school onwards.

The Rugby Football Union has a keen sense of the importance of good coaching and operates many courses and conferences throughout the year to improve the standard of coaching.

This book has been prepared as an introduction to the game and rules of Rugby Union. With expert coaching you will learn the skills of the game and enjoy the thrill of match play.

Full details on all aspects of Rugby Football can be obtained from:

Don Rutherford
Technical Administrator
Rugby Football Union
Whitton Road
Twickenham TW2 7RG

Part 1

Introduction to the Game

1 A thrilling dramatic sight wherever Rugby is played. A player diving over the line for a try – the climax stemming from a combined team effort.

2 But for this youngster, proudly trying his team jersey for size, that try is still in the future;

3 something he will be striving to achieve in this, his first match.

4 But let us leave our newcomer to Rugby for a moment and go back to the year 1823, to Rugby school in England, and to the boy who is generally regarded as the founder of the game, William Webb Ellis.

5 At the age of 15, playing 'football' in a match between Rugby and Bigside, William Webb Ellis broke the rules then in existence, by picking up the ball and running with it.

6 100 years later, a tablet in the wall of Rugby Close was unveiled. It reads: "This stone commemorates the exploit of William Webb Ellis, who, with a fine disregard for the rules of football as played in his time, first took the ball in his arms and ran with it, thus originating the distinctive feature of the Rugby game. A.D. 1823".

7 Development of the game as we know it today, was slow, although the Rugby School brand of football spread to the universities of Oxford and Cambridge. The undergraduates of these universities were to become devotees of the game.

8 When they graduated, the university students became ambassadors for the code, and, as doctors and teachers, introduced Rugby to hospitals and schools. Clubs were formed, the oldest of which are Blackheath and Guys Hospital.

9 Gradually, the image of the game emerged, and to-day its laws are standardised by the International Rugby Football Board.

10 But, to return to Rugby's newest recruit - one of the fifteen players who constitute a team. The number on the player's jersey is for identification by spectators and usually denotes his position on the field of play

11 Boots are a most important item of a player's equipment. He should constantly check them for defects in the leather, making sure that the studs (be they aluminium, nylon or leather are in perfect condition.

12 A most important man on the field of play the referee, is entitled to order a player to remove any part of his football gear which in the referee's opinion, may cause injury to another player. (These sharp edges or worn aluminium studs are certainly no acceptable, and in fact, are dangerous.)

13 Now our newcomer to the game runs on to the field for his first match:

14 a match in which he will *catch, pass* and sometimes *kick* this ball.

15 Wherever possible, the field of play is 110 yards long and 75 yards wide. Obviously, younger teams often play on a smaller field and use a smaller ball.

16 The half-way mark is the line on which play begins.

17 On each side of the field there is a broken line five yards in from the touch line, which runs the length of the playing area. This is called the five yard line.

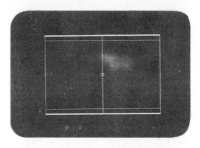

18 In each half there is a broken line (running across the pitch) ten yards from the half-way mark.

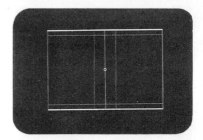

19 Twenty-five yards from each end con-tinuous lines are drawn across the pitch. These are the 25-yard lines.

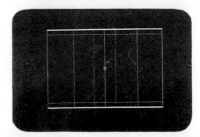

20 At each end of the field, and in the centre of the goal line, are the goal posts. They measure ten feet from the ground to the top edge of the crossbar, and eighteen feet six inches between the insides of the posts.

21 Behind each goal line an area, not exceeding twenty-five yards in length, is known as the in-goal area. The end of it is marked by the dead ball line.

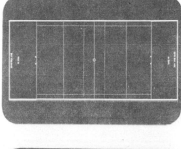

22 The four corners of the field are marked by corner posts, which are usually made of pliable materials, so that a player crashing into them will not be injured.

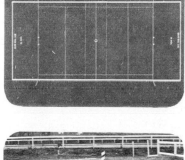

23 These posts should be at least four feet in height.

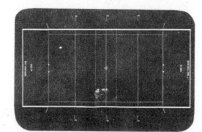

24 The points at which the half-way line and the 25-yard lines meet the touch-line or side lines are marked by flag posts set well outside the field of play. This then is the field on which our match is to take place. In senior Rugby, the game lasts for two halves, up to forty minutes each, but for youngsters the playing time is generally much less.

25   Half-time is a period of not more than five minutes, during which both teams remain on the field. For the second half the teams change ends.

26   The aim of each team is to win the match by scoring as many points as possible. Points are scored by grounding the ball over the opponents' goal line, but not necessarily between the goal posts, in what is referred to as a *try;*

27   and by kicking the ball between the opposition goal posts, *above* the cross bar. This is called a *goal.*

28   After scoring a *try,* counting four points, the team *kicks at goal* to convert the four points to six, the successful goal kick counting *two* points. A goal scored from a free kick, a penalty kick, or a drop kick, gives 3 points. A goal scored during the course of play with the use of the *drop* kick is termed a dropped goal.

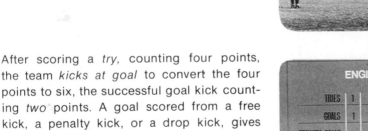

	ENGLAND	FRANCE		
TRIES	1	4		
GOALS	1	2		
PENALTY GOALS			2	6
TOTAL	6		6	

29   We have already mentioned the importance of the referee, who ensures that both teams play the game fairly in accordance with the laws. It is interesting to observe the referee's position during the game.

30 He is not only in sole charge of the match, but acts as timekeeper as well as keeping the score.

31 He gives his services voluntarily to Rugby, and it is the responsibility of every player to respect his actions and to accept his decisions with good grace.

32 To assist the referee, there are two touch judges, equipped with flags, with which they signal whenever the ball crosses the touch lines and so goes out of play, or into touch – in fact, to determine at what point on the side line play will resume, and to show which side will throw the ball in.

33 When a penalty or *free kick at goal* is being taken, the referee orders the touch judges behind the goal to signal whether the kick was successful;

34 or to flag an unsuccessful kick away. The touch judges are generally in a better position than the referee to decide whether or not the ball has passed between the goal posts and over the cross bar. But the referee is in charge of the game. He may disagree with the touch judges and over-rule their verdict. His is the final say.

35 There are no hard and fast rules governing the positions of the fifteen players who make up a team, but let us, briefly, at this stage, examine the players' functions. First, the full back, No. 15: a strong kicker with either foot, a reliable tackler and the ability to run from keep positions;

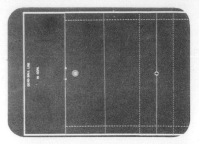

36 the two wingers, left No. 11, and right No. 14;

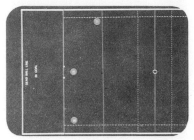

37 the two centres, No. 12 and No. 13;

38 the outside half, No. 10, and scrum half, No. 9;

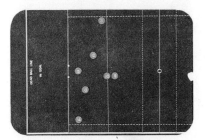

39 and the forwards – eight of them made up of the No. 8;

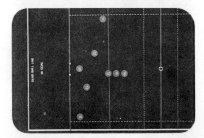

40 the four second-row players (right and left flanker, No. 7 and No. 6, and two lock forwards, No. 4 and No. 5);

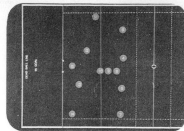

41 ....and finally the two props, No. 1 and No. 3, and the hooker, No. 2.

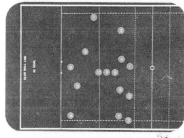

42 Before the match begins, one captain tosses a coin in front of the referee. The other captain calls. The winner *may* elect to *kick off*, choose *the goal line he intends to defend*, or whether to run *with* or *against* the sun or wind. After half-time, the *kick off* is taken by the team which did not kick off to start the game.

43 But already our newcomer to the game is aware of two vital factors that can only add to a player's efficiency. First, each and every player's smart appearance. Admittedly, a smart team is not *necessarily* a good team, but a good team is *invariably* neatly and safely turned out.

44 Secondly, and even more important, our young player will learn that physical fitness is the key to success on the field. He has learnt to develop his physique and the effective use of his body.

45   Fitness. Knowledge. Combine these, and you will enjoy every moment of the game.

Questionnaire Part 1

1.   Who founded the game of Rugby Union and when?

2.   How many players are there in a Rugby Union team?

3.   What size is a normal Rugby Union pitch?

4.   Where does play begin?

5.   What are the markings on a Rugby Union pitch?

6.   What are the dimensions of the goal posts?

7.   What are the boundaries of the in-goal area?

8.   How long does a game of Rugby Union last?

9.   How are points scored?

10.   What are the duties of the referee and touch judges?

Part 2

Passing and Handling the Ball

1 We left our rival captains tossing a coin in the presence of the referee.

2 The captain of the red team (having won the toss) has elected to run with the wind for the first half, and invites the black team to take the kick off.

3 The match is about to begin.

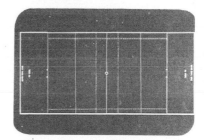

4 Having chosen to attack the left hand goal line, the captain of the red team positions his players as demonstrated here – spread out in an open pattern to receive the ball from the kick off.

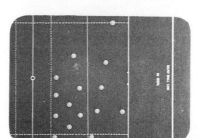

5   Observe the difference in the positioning of the black team; the forwards lined out across the field; the backs ready to attack.

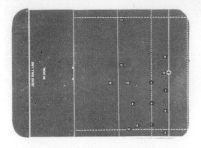

6   The ball is placed in the centre of the half-way line and a place kick is taken by the nominated black player, in this case No. 12.

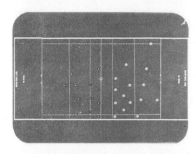

7   The ball is kicked forward beyond the red team's ten yard line (unless a member of the red team plays the ball before it reaches the ten yard line, in which case play is allowed to continue). The black team remain behind the half way line and the red players must stand within their ten yard line until the ball has been kicked.

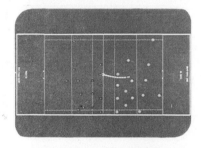

8   It is impossible to make a constructive move with the rugby ball until we have learnt to hold it correctly. Fingers splayed comfortably around the centre seam, holding it firmly and effectively with the whole of the surface area of both hands. Practise holding the ball in this way and move it about in front of the body.

9   Having learnt how to hold the ball correctly, study and practise the art of *passing*. This is passing to the left.

10 The ball pointing to the ground, the feet comfortably placed not too far apart; with the head and eyes turned towards the receiver of the pass, the arms swung in the direction of the receiver. Final delivery of the ball is controlled by the fingers.

11 The speed of a pass is governed by the distance between two players so that the ball travels parallel to the ground to a point just beyond the receiver. Not too fast – not too slow – just right.

12 In making a pass to the right when standing, the same principles apply in reverse.

13 Before attempting a pass on the run you will need to learn the correct way of running with the ball. It is carried in both hands in front of the body. The reasons for this, are that the ball is perfectly positioned for a pass either to right or left, and when you hold the ball like this the opposition is uncertain of your next move.

14 If the ball is tucked under one arm, the defence will come in for the tackle, as our newcomer to Rugby has discovered in his first match. The red player here has tackled confidently, knowing that, with the ball tucked under his arm, the black player has no time to get rid of it.

15 The fundamentals of passing the ball on the run are identical to those of the standing pass. The difference lies in knowing *when,* and *off which foot,* to pass.

16 *Remember* – eyes on the ball all the time.

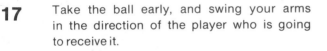

17 Take the ball early, and swing your arms in the direction of the player who is going to receive it.

18 The ability to catch a rugby ball from a high kick is a skill that can only be acquired with constant practise. This player is perfectly positioned, both arms are extended above the head, and forward, acting as *sighters,* and with eyes glued to the ball, the player's hands literally enclose its path through the air.

19 As his outstretched fingers make contact he is still watching it closely.

20 As he pulls the ball in he hunches his shoulders: wrists close together to bring the bent elbows in towards the body: chest pulled in: in fact, he makes a basket or cradle for the ball with hands, shoulders, chest and elbows. Only when the ball is safely cradled in this way can he afford to take his eyes off it.

21 To prevent the ball rebounding from his chest to the ground, both hands are brought over the top of it and the catch is complete.

22 Perhaps the most difficult ball to retrieve is the rolling ball. By bending down, the entire bulk of the body is presented to the oncoming ball – hands correctly positioned and eyes on the ball, as they must be if it is to be taken cleanly.

23 But with his first match behind him now, our newcomer to the game has . himself applied some of the skills learnt on the practise field.

Questionnaire Part 2

1. What choices does a team captain have when he wins the toss?

2. To commence play what type of kick is used?

3.　　Where is the first kick taken from?

4.　　Where must the ball land after the first kick?

5.　　What happens if the first kick is intercepted before it lands?

6.　　Where must the opposition players stand when the first kick is taken?

7.　　How is the ball held whilst running?

8.　　Describe a method of passing the ball.

9.　　Why should you not carry the ball under one arm?

10.　　How do you catch the ball after a high kick?

Part 3

Kicking

1 Wherever Rugby is played, the boots of Don Clarke are respected, so let us study his instruction in the art of kicking the ball.

2 First, the *place kick*. Here we see the round hole method of placing the ball for the upright place kick. There is also the banked method of placing the ball, but whichever method is used, the inside of the hole must be smooth. A bump on one side of the hole will affect the ball's flight and the accuracy of the kick.

3 The hole is dug out with the heel to a depth of an inch to an inch and a half. If the same depth of hole is used for every place kick, there is no variation in the point of impact (the point at which the kicker's boot meets the ball).

4 The round hole is used where the kicker prefers the ball upright. The banked hole is used for the slanted or angled ball.

5 The flatter position of the ball is frequently used for long kicks, although Don Clarke does all his kicking with the ball in the upright position. During his long career in top-class rugby, he has obtained greater *distance* and *accuracy* with the *upright* ball but this may not be every kicker's experience.

6 No matter which of the two positions you prefer, the placing of the ball is most important. For a right foot kicker the centre seam is in line with the right leg; the lacing on the far side of the ball.

7 Observe how for a *right* foot *place kick at goal* the centre seam of the ball is lined up on the right leg and the centre of the cross bar.

8 When there is a wind blowing across field, allow for it by *laying off* like this. By lining up the ball on the far goal post you allow for the wind to swing the ball in and through the posts, above the cross bar.

9 With the right leg and foot behind the centre seam, the *left* boot is positioned some four to six inches behind and to one side of the ball for a right foot kick. At the end of the run-up the *left* foot will attempt to come to rest in this position, allowing the right foot to swing through and connect cleanly. This is extremely important.

10 Experience has taught Don Clarke that where the ball is to be kicked from 15 to 20 yards out, a walk back of two to three paces is sufficient. But, for anything beyond this distance, he recommends a walk back of six or seven paces, to relax, gain confidence and balance. *But, of course, the distance can be varied as the kicker chooses.*

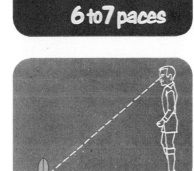

11 As he walks back, his eyes are fixed not just on the ball, but on the spot about an inch to an inch and a half from the ground with which his right foot will make contact.

12 Still watching that spot, he takes his first step forward. A slow step to make sure he is balanced, and running in straight. Confident that he is perfectly balanced and that he is not running off line, he moves through to kick the ball truly.

13 As he moves closer to the ball, he eyes gradually travel up the ball to the top of the straight back seam.

14 And the right foot comes through to make contact, with the left foot correctly positioned.

15 The number of paces required for the place kick will vary with individual players, but the run-up must be relaxed: no stops and starts – an easy balanced approach that enables the kicker to concentrate his energy on the kick itself.

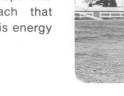

16 Some players prefer to take their line on the ball at the end of the walk back from it, in the belief that concentration is sometimes lost in keeping the eyes glued to it from the moment the ball is placed in the hole.

17 Whichever method you choose, the essential requirement is to keep your eyes on the ball once it has been lined up.

18 In successful place kicking, the area approximately two feet in front of the kick, and some twelve inches beyond it, is of vital importance. Here we see Don Clarke, perfectly balanced, body square on to the ball, prepared to give it what he terms a – *thump*.

19 As he follows through on the kick, his body momentum carries him about a yard past the spot where the ball was placed, before his right foot touches the ground. There is no exaggerated lifting of the kicking foot to gain elevation of the ball. It is being kicked from the ground so it will rise on its own if it is properly struck.

20 It is the combination of body momentum and that *thump* he mentions, that enables Don Clarke to kick the ball fifty to sixty yards with almost monotonous precision.

21 Lining the ball up correctly. Co-ordination. Balance. Eyes on the ball. The correct placement of the non-kicking foot. Concentration. The ability to be oblivious of everything but the kick to be taken.

22 These are the fundamentals which, when allied with *constant practise,* produce the perfect *place kick.*

23 For the *punt* or *torpedo* kick, the hands cradle the ball as shown here – the lacing on top. For a right foot punt, the ball is held diagonally across the front of the body from right to left.

24 For a left foot punt (and it is a tremendous advantage to be able to punt with either foot) the reverse applies.

25 Here we see Don Clarke, perfectly balanced, prior to punting for the touch line.

26 The ball is not thrown but dropped, on to the instep of the kicking foot – dropped well forward so that contact is made as the leg straightens.

27 The only time a Rugby ball should be kicked with the toe of the boot is when it is lying on the ground at the moment of impact. Here, when *contact* is *made,* the whole length of the top of the boot is in contact with the ball.

28 Here the kicker has kept his head down, *watching the ball* from the moment he decided to punt, this time with the left foot. Again there is no exaggerated follow through, merely a concentrated effort on that *thump.*

29 As with the punt, the position of the hands cradling the ball is an important factor in the success of the *drop kick.*

30 The ball is dropped well forward of the body, on *end.*

31 The position of the hands governs the drop of the ball, which is leaning slightly back towards the kicking foot.

32 As the ball bounces, the foot comes through, toe pointed to the ground, and the ball is kicked with the instep.

33 A player is entitled to drop kick in the field of play, and if he succeeds in getting it over the bar between the posts he scores 3 points for his team. Obviously the chances of error are considerably greater than with a *place kick;* but if the ball comes loose, and the kicker is in the clear, a drop goal is a tremendous morale booster.

34 To attempt drop goals from every position on the field is a waste of time; but the unexpectedness, when the player is correctly positioned within kicking distance of the goal, brings its own reward.

35   Again, the head is down watching the ball. The kicker is balanced as he follows through on the kick.

36   And (as he has proved frequently in Rugby Internationals) Don Clarke is dangerously adept at drop kicking goals.

37   Practise with both left and right foot kicking. The player who can kick with either foot is of much greater value to his team.

38   The advice of Don Clarke, New Zealand International, is: "First learn the correct technique and then practise, practise and more practise if you want to achieve perfection".

Questionnaire Part 3

1.   How would you prepare the ground for a place kick?

2.   When would you use a banked hole?

3.   How would you position the ball for a place kick?

4.   Where should the left foot be positioned for a right foot kick?

5.   What is a punt kick?

6.   How is the ball held for a punt kick?

7.   When should a rugby ball be kicked with the toe of the boot?

8.   What is a drop kick?

9.   Which part of the foot should touch the ball in a drop kick?

10.   When may a drop kick be taken?

Part 4

The Referee - Kick off - Knock on - Scrummage

1 Of all sport's officials, surely the most maligned, misjudged and unappreciated is the Rugby referee.

2 Whenever he blows his whistle – and sometimes when he does not – he incurs the wrath of the supporters of one side or the other.

3 But this is his lot. If he is to be a referee he must accept it philosophically, applying without fear or favour his expert knowledge of the laws of Rugby with sympathetic humour, regardless of the counsel of partisan spectators – whom Kipling might well have described as muddled dopes.

4 From this heartening introduction to your thankless task, let us push on to an examination of the laws, and the referee's responsibilities.

5   The referee's uniform consists of jersey, shorts and long socks. To avoid confusion to players and spectators, he should select an entirely different colour from that of either team.

6   He carries a whistle, watch, paper and pencil.

7   He must ensure that no player is wearing illegal equipment, such as shoulder harness, although sewn-in rubber or cotton wool may be worn as protective pads – with the referee's sanction.

8   Dangerous rings

9   and jagged boot studs are illegal and could injure other players.

10   The referee should consider and understand the advantage law.

11   Let us define the laws, beginning with the kick-off. A place kick is taken at the centre of the half-way line: to start a match, to resume play after half time, and after *any type of goal* has been scored.

KICK - OFF

12   A drop kick is taken (at or behind the centre of the half-way line) after an unconverted try.

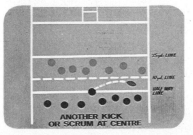

13   All players of the team kicking off must be behind the ball when it is kicked. If any player is not, the referee orders a scrummage at the centre of the half-way line.

14   From the kick-off, the ball must reach the 10-yard line, unless *first* played by an opponent. If the ball fails to go 10 yards forward, the non-kicking team has the option of having the ball kicked off again or taking a scrum in the centre.

25yd. LINE
10yd. LINE
HALF WAY LINE

ANOTHER KICK
OR SCRUM AT CENTRE

15 The ball is kicked off again if any of the non-kicking team stand within 10 yards of the half-way line, or if any of the opposing team charge before the kicker's foot makes contact with the ball, or if the wrong type of kick is taken.

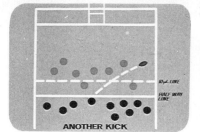

16 A goal cannot be scored from the kick-off. If the ball pitches in touch, touch-in-goal, or on or over the dead ball line, the referee gives the opposing side the option of another kick-off, by the same side, a scrummage in the centre, or accepting the kick.

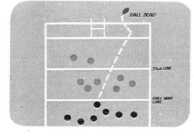

17 But if the ball *pitches in goal* and then becomes dead, the referee will award the opposing side a drop-out. We will deal with the drop-out later.

18 We come now to the knock-on. A ball is knocked on if it travels from a player's hand or arm in the direction of the opponents' dead-ball line.

19 It is not ruled as a knock-on if the player retains effective control of it.

except when intercepting an opponent's pass

21 or if a player propels it forward accidentally,

22 and does not allow it to touch the ground or another player when catching it direct from a kick or pass.

23 The ball is said to be *thrown forward* – called a forward pass – if the player in possession throws it in the direction of the opponents' dead-ball line.

THROW FORWARD

24 There are two types of scrummage – a ruck and a set scrum. A ruck is formed when one or more players from each team, on their feet in the field of play, are in physical contact while the ball is on the ground between them.

SCRUMMAGING

25 A set scrum is formed when players of each team close up in the field of play in readiness for the ball to be put on the ground between them. The laws specify that no player may

26 intentionally collapse a scrummage

27 intentionally fall or kneel in any scrummage

28 handle the ball in any scrummage

29 return the ball to any scrummage after it has come out.

30 Any player on the ground where a scrummage is formed must not interfere with the ball and must try to roll away from it.

31 In a set scrummage three players from each side form their respective front rows. They bind together, so that none has his arms around another's neck, and that his hands are at or below his neighbour's armpits.

32 When the two front rows come together their heads dovetail. In other words, no player in the front row has his head next to that of a team-mate.

33 The left arm of the loose-head prop is inside that of his immediate opponent – the opposing side's tight head prop.

✗ 34 A scrummage cannot be delayed because a player has not got his head down.

35 The scrummage must be as stationary as possible while awaiting the ball, and must be so formed that the mid-line of the tunnel is parallel to the goal lines. Incidentally, the "mid-line" is that formed on the ground by the line of the junction of the shoulders of the two front rows and *not* the mid-distance between the two lines of feet.

36 When a scrummage is near a goal line the defending side's front row must have their feet in the field of play.

37 The player putting in the ball must do so from the side he *first* chooses. He cannot change his mind and go around to the other side.

38 The player putting the ball into the scrummage stands *one yard* from the scrum and, with both hands, throws the ball in midway between the front rows. This is a *single* forward movement from a level midway between his knee and ankle.

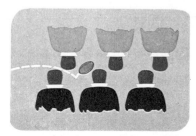

39 The ball should pitch *on the ground*, at least as far as the loose head prop's inner shoulder.

40 The front row's feet are placed to allow a clear tunnel, so that the ball can get into the scrummage correctly.

41 No front row player of either side may raise or advance a foot until the ball touches the ground. Then any foot of the front row players may strike for the ball.

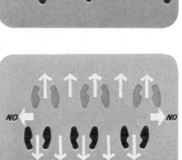

42 The ball may legally be heeled between any two feet in the scrummage but *not* through either end of the tunnel.

43 No player may raise both his feet off the ground at the same time, twist or lower his body, or adopt any position liable to cause the scrummage to collapse – such as advancing both his feet into the opposing second row.

THIS IS ILLEGAL

• 44 The referee stands on the side of the scrummage from which the ball is being put in.

45 When the ball has been won, the referee stands up at once to watch the loose forwards on the far side of the scrummage. Loose forwards commonly commit the breach of breaking from the scrum before the ball is out. Watch for it.

Questionnaire Part 4

1. What is the advantage law?

2. When is a place kick taken?

3. When and where is a drop kick taken?

4. What action would a referee take if one of the players of the team kicking off was in front of the ball?

5. What happens if the ball does not reach the ten yard line after the kick off?

6. When is a kick off taken again?

7. What does the referee do if the ball pitches over the dead ball line after a kick off?

8. What is a knock on?

9. What is a ruck and a maul?

10. How is the ball put into the scrummage?

5 This is not a tackle, so he may pass the ball;

6 or he may get up and continue to run with the ball. Whatever happens he may not just lie on the ball.

7 When tackled, a player must immediately release the ball, and no other player may prevent him from doing so.

8 No tackled player (or tackler lying on the ground after a tackle) may interfere with the ball in any way. This tackler, after bringing down his opponent, and while still on the ground, tries to dive on the rolling ball. That is illegal.

9 This is the correct method of releasing the ball in a "stand up" tackle.

10 and after a low tackle.

11 A tackled player's momentum...

12 may carry him from the field of play, over the goal line to score a try. But it *must* be only MOMENTUM, not a second movement.

13● Frequently after a tackle, an inconclusive maul develops. If the referee has doubts as to who failed to release the ball he awards a scrum to the side not responsible for stoppage of play. If he cannot decide, he gives the scrum to the team moving forward prior to the stoppage; but if neither side was moving forward, to the defending side.

14 As soon as he decides the ball is unplayable, he blows his whistle.

15 When a ruck is formed after a player has fallen on the ground, the player must release the ball immediately.

16 Let us consider the off-side law.

17 Rugby's off-side laws are clear and specific. In open play, a player is off-side if he is in front of a team-mate who last played the ball. Here red player A is carrying the ball towards the goal-line. His team-mates B and C are clearly off-side.

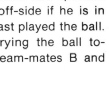

18 A player who is off-side is out of the game: he may not play the ball or interfere in any way with an opponent. He is literally off-the-side.

19 A referee should not necessarily penalise a player who finds himself in an off-side position. A player who receives a forward pass is not penalised for off-side, since the throw forward is the first infringement committed.

20 A player is not penalised just for being in an off-side position unless he interferes with the ball or an opponent – with three exceptions: in scrums, in line-outs, and remaining within 10 yards of a player waiting to receive the ball. This black player is waiting within 10 yards of the red player receiving a ball kicked by another red player.

21 The only way he can avoid a penalty is by getting quickly outside the 10 yard radius.

22 The off-side player who is not retiring cannot be put *on-side* by an action of his opponents, such as a fumble, running with the ball, passing or kicking it.

23 Apart from the off-side player within 10 yards of an opponent waiting to receive the ball, a player may be put on-side in general play when

24 an opponent intentionally touches the ball but fails to gather it (note *intentionally touches* – there must be an intent to field the ball)

25   or an opponent carrying the ball has run at least five yards,

26   or an opponent kicks the ball,

27   or passes it,

28   or the kicker (or player of his team behind him) runs in front of his off-side team-mate.

29   A player who last kicked the ball may follow up *in touch* but he must be in the field of play at the moment he puts his own player on-side. Here player A has kicked the ball, followed through, and put team-mate B *on-side* after re-entering the field of play.

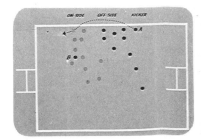

30 The referee should whistle when an off-side player continues to charge within 10 yards of an opponent waiting to play the ball. If the non-offending side gains no advantage, the referee awards a penalty kick, with the option of a scrummage. If the ball was played in-goal, the scrummage will be five yards from the goal-line from the position where the ball was last played.

Questionnaire Part 5

1. What is a tackle?

2. What does the referee do if it is not clear which team held on to the ball after a tackle?

3. How does the referee signal that the ball is unplayable?

4. When is a player "off-side"?

5. When would a referee penalise a player for being off-side?

6. How can a player put himself back on-side?

7. How can a player be put back on-side by action of the opposing team?

8. How can a player be put back on-side by a team-mate?

9. What penalty does a referee award when a player is off-side?

10. What choice of penalty does the non-offending side have?

Part 6

Off-side in Scrums and Line-outs

1   In Rugby scrums and line-outs, the off-side laws are slightly different from those in open play, which we have already examined.

2   A player is off-side if he enters a set scrum or ruck from his opponents' side. In a ruck he must enter from his own side, and bind with a player of his own team.

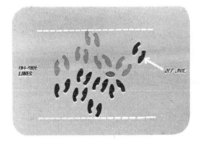

3   At a set scrum, an imaginary line drawn through the hindmost foot of the players on each side is called the scrummage off-side line. All players not in the scrummage are off-side if they fail to retire quickly behind this line while the ball is in the scrum, except the man putting in the ball and his opposite number.

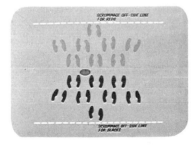

4   Any player not in the set scrum, excluding those putting in the ball for their respective teams, is off-side if he advances or remains behind the off-side line while the ball is in the scrum.

5   Both players who put the ball into the set scrum for their teams (usually the half-backs) may follow the ball through the scrum. But neither may move his foot in front of the ball as this would make him off-side.

6   Any player, except the front row, may leave the scrummage while the ball is still in, *provided* he is behind the ball and retires *immediately* behind the hindmost foot. So, loose forwards may break, but must retire at once behind the off-side line.

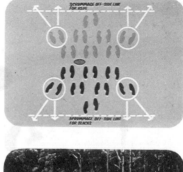

7   A player is not in the scrum unless he is binding with at least one arm around the body of one of his own players.

8   Clinging to a team-mate's jersey or arm, or placing a hand on the scrum, is not binding.

9   This is a maul, which is the same as a ruck, except that the ball is held up, and not on the ground.

10   A player is off-side if he enters a ruck or maul from the opponents' side. The offending player is indicated by the arrow.

11   Any player not in the ruck or maul *retires behind the ball without delay*

12   then joins the ruck or maul from *behind* the ball,

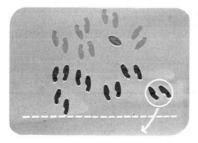

13   or retires behind the scrummage off-side line, as indicated by the arrow.

● 14   The off-side line for all those not taking part in the ruck or maul is a line through the hindmost foot and parallel to the goal line. No player, including the half-back, may follow the ball through a ruck or maul.

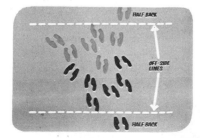

15 This is a properly formed ruck, with no loiterers waiting for their opponents to heel the ball.

16 Players who are retiring as quickly as they can to the scrummage off-side line are put on-side, when one of their opponents has run five yards, carrying the ball;

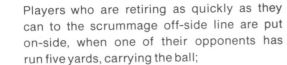

17 or has kicked the ball.

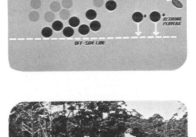

18 The off-side players are *not* put on-side, after a ruck, by their opponents passing the ball. In this situation they continue to retire until an opponent kicks the ball or carries it five yards.

19 This player is penalised because he has joined in the play, or interfered with an opponent, before he is on-side.

20 Now let us examine the off-side law for line-outs – and it should be understood that it is not necessary to have a line-out to bring the ball back into play. If a quick throw-in is correctly taken, the line-out laws do not apply. If a quick throw-in is not taken, then a line-out is formed.

21 First we should be clear about what a line-out is, when it starts, when it finishes, who is taking part, and who is not.

22 The law says that a line-out is a formation of at least two players of each side, lining up in single parallel lines in readiness for the ball to be thrown in between them.

23 Obviously, this line-out is illegal. The players have not formed single parallel lines.

24 The line-out extends from player A to the position of the furthest player taking part in the line-out, player B. The last player, joining the end of the line-out, should belong to the team throwing in the ball. Black team are throwing in, so no red player may stand beyond B.

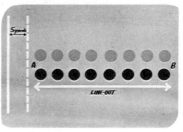

25   The line-out starts when the ball leaves
the hands of the player throwing it in.

26   The line-out ends when one of these situ-
ations occurs.

(7) The line-out ends when
  • the ball is on the ground and a ruck has
    been formed, or
  • a player carrying the ball leaves the line-
    out, or
  • the ball has been passed or knocked back
    from the line-out, or
  • the ball is thrown beyond the furthest
    player, or
  • a maul is taking place and all feet of
    players in the maul have moved beyond
    the line-of-touch, or
  • the ball becomes unplayable.

27   This maul does not end the line-out unless
all the feet of the players have moved beyond
the line-of-touch.

28   The only players who are in the line-out are
those taking up their positions on each side
of the imaginary line between their files, in
readiness to receive the ball. This imaginary
line is called the line-of-touch.

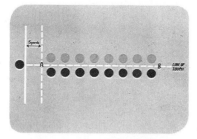

29   The players leave a clear space between
their two files and remain on their own side
of the line-of-touch until the ball has touched
a player or the ground except.

30 when actually jumping for the ball. A player who crosses the line in jumping for the ball, but failing to get it, is not penalised. *But he should make an effort to get back on his own side.* In any case, he should not use another player as a support to enable him to jump for the ball.

31 When the ball has touched the ground, or one of the line-out men, then all players keep *behind the ball.* A player is allowed to tackle an opponent who has caught the ball, provided the tackle starts from his own side of the line.

32 Remember: only the players who line up in readiness for the ball to be thrown in are said to be participating in the line-out. No other player may move beyond the last man in the line-out at the moment the ball is thrown in, except for the purpose of catching the ball in the case of a long throw in.

33 Any man who is part of the line-out may move towards or away from the touch line, provided he keeps close to the line-of-touch a process called peeling off.

34 The arrow indicates a player peeling off correctly, and after he has received the ball. The line-out has consequently ended.

35 Once in the line-out, a player may not leave it until it ends. Until then he may not retreat towards his own goal line.

Questionnaire Part 6

1.   From which side must a player enter a scrummage?

2.   Where is the off-side line in a scrummage?

3.   What is a maul?

4.   Where is the off-side line for a ruck or maul?

5.   How are players put on-side in a ruck or maul?

6.   What is a line out?

7.   When is a line out formed?

8.   How far does a line out extend?

9.   When does a line out start and end?

10.   How do you decide which players are in the line out?

Part 7

The Line-out

1 We have seen what a line-out is, who takes part in it and how the off-side laws apply to it. Now let us see how these laws affect players *not* participating in the line-out.

2 We should understand that the backs (who do not habitually take part in line-outs, or scrums) may not join a line-out at any stage. From start to finish of a line-out, the backs (excluding the half-backs) may not approach within 10 yards of the line-of-touch. There is one exception which we will see later.

3 Even if a maul develops, the backs remain 10 yards away because, as we have seen, a maul does not end the line-out unless it moves completely from the line-of-touch.

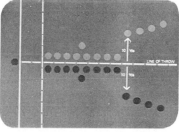

4 When a line-out is within 10 yards of the goal-line, the backs should remain on the goal-line until the line-out is finished.

5 The only occasion on which backs *are* permitted to advance beyond the so-called line-out off-side line is when a long throw-in sends the ball beyond the last line-out man. In these circumstances, backs of both sides may advance in an attempt to field the ball as soon as it leaves the hands of the player throwing it in.

6 But if they advance in anticipation, and the ball fails to reach the furthest player in the line-out, they must be penalised.

7 Four players are excluded from the 10 yard restriction area at line-outs. They are the players of each side who normally receive the ball from the line-out (usually the half backs), and the man throwing in the ball and his immediate opponent (usually the blind side winger).

8 The half-back may operate anywhere within the 10 yard area provided he does not stand or move beyond the last man in the line-out before the ball has passed that man.

9 Only when the ball has passed the last man may the half-back advance beyond him.

10 Now let us look at the line-out role of the player throwing in the ball and his immediate opponent. During the line-out he should do one of four things: (a) after throwing in, he remains within five yards of the touch line;

11 ...or he retreats to the 10 yard restriction line – 10 yards back from the line of touch;

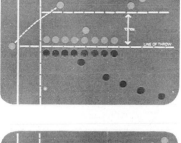

12 or he joins the line-out;

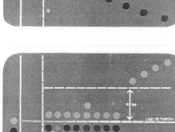

13 or he moves into position to receive the ball from the line-out - that is to say he becomes an acting half-back *provided the original half-back has retreated to the 10 yard restriction line* before the line-out has formed.

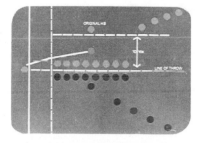

14 For any infringement occuring within the line-out, the referee awards a penalty kick 15 yards infield along the line-of-touch.

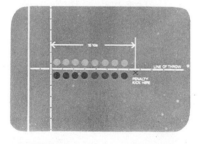

15 If the offender is peeling, or moving beyond the farthest player in the line illegally, or the offender is one not taking part in the line-out as shown, the referee awards the player nearest the referee the penalty kick on the offending team's off-side line opposite the place of infringement, but not less than 15 yards from the touch-line.

16 Now let us look at some general line-out laws. The ball is thrown in by an opponent of the last player to touch, kick or carry the ball into touch. The throw-in is against a player pushed into touch while carrying the ball.

17 The two men in front of the line-out stand on or beyond the five yard line, and the ball is thrown in so as to touch a player or the ground at least five yards infield. Otherwise the referee gives the opposing side the option of throwing in, or having a set scrum 15 yards infield on the line-of-touch.

18 If the referee considers that any player wilfully prevents the ball travelling five yards from the throw-in, he awards a penalty kick 15 yards infield on the line-of-touch.

19 The ball is thrown in so that it touches a player or the ground on a line at right angles to the touch line. If it is not, the referee gives the opposing team the option of throwing in or taking a scrummage 15 yards infield. Do not forget that the advantage law applies to the so called crooked throw.

20 When the same infringement occurs a second time in one line out the referee orders a scrummage 15 yards infield (again on the line of touch) with the non-offending side to put in the ball.

scrummage for same infringement twice in one line-out.
non offenders put in the ball

21 The player throwing in keeps both feet out of the field of play. He may throw the ball any way he likes, provided that it travels straight for five yards and touches a player or the ground on a line at right angles to the touch line.

22 Remember, it is not necessary to have a line-out every time the ball goes into touch. The thrower-in need not wait for his team-mates to arrive. *Anyone* can throw in the ball to any player on the spot; he can even throw it in to himself.

23 But he must be a member of the team entitled to the throw-in; throw it from the correct spot; at least five yards, at right angles to the touch line.

24 In the case of a quick throw in, he should regain the ball himself. If a quick throw in is not taken a line-out is formed when the ball goes into touch. When this occurs *all the line-out off-side laws should be observed.* In the line-out the referee should be on his guard against common offences.

25 Loitering should not be tolerated; all players should make rapid attempts to get on-side. Nevertheless, the thrower-in need not wait for them to get on-side.

26 Every experienced referee and player knows that the line-out is a breeding ground of all manner of obstruction and unfair practices, which in turn produce ill-temper, malice and similar uncharitable qualities. Two of these illegal practices often, alas, escape the notice of referees. For example:

27 It is illegal for any player to use any other player as a prop to lever himself upward as he jumps.

28 It is illegal for a player to hold another down to prevent him jumping for the ball, by grasping his jersey or stamping on his foot.

29 No player may hold any other of *either team* before the ball has touched the line-out or the ground. Thus, hoisting a team-mate to help him reach higher, is positively illegal.

30 If there are troubles in the line-out it may help to ask (or insist) that the space between the two lines of forwards be wider.

31 Deal promptly and firmly with line-out breaches. If you let the players know at once that you will not tolerate rough stuff or deliberate illegalities you help to produce a free-flowing, fast-moving game as Rugby is meant to be.

Questionnaire Part 7

1. Where must the backs position themselves during the line-out?

2. When a line-out is within ten yards of the goal line, where should the defending backs remain until the line-out is finished?

3. When may backs advance beyond the line-out off-side line?

4. Who are the four players excluded from the ten yard restriction area in a line-out?

5. In a line-out, what are the four positions the player throwing the ball can move to after throwing in?

6. Where will a penalty kick be taken for infringements in the line-out?

7. Who throws in the ball in a line-out?

8. Where do the front two men in the line-out stand?

9. What is the alternative to a line-out?

10. What are two illegal practices that must be watched for in the line-out?

Part 8

Duties of the Referee and Touch Judges

1   We have seen what the Rugby referee wears and that his equipment includes a whistle and a reliable watch.

2   We know, too, that he exercises great care in prohibiting dangerous garb on the field.

3   It is well to remember that he also keeps the score. For this he should not rely on his memory, or the score-board, but carry a small card and pencil to jot down the progressive scores.

4   A try is scored by grounding the ball in the opponents' in-goal, counting 4 points. When a try-at-goal is successful, a further 2 points are awarded. A goal from a free kick, a penalty kick or a dropped goal scores 3 points. A scoreboard might read: 7 tries 28 points; 3 converted tries 6 points; 1 goal 3 points; making a total score of 37.

TRIES	7	28
GOALS	4	9
		37

5 In his judgement (as in all other aspects) the referee must stick to the laws. He may not vary or refuse to enforce any law in any circumstances.

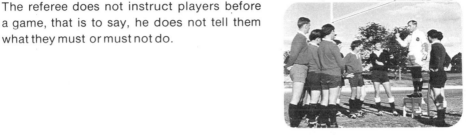

6 The referee does not instruct players before a game, that is to say, he does not tell them what they must or must not do.

7 Obviously, during a game, he cannot accept anyone else's opinion about facts. He is the sole judge of fact and time, although he may consult the touch judges on matters concerning their functions.

8 An important duty of the referee is to give the players a clear reason why he has blown his whistle. This helps the players to observe the laws, and makes for better understanding between players and referee.

9 Only *players* are allowed to enter the playing enclosure. Benevolent spectators (there *are* a few!) must not be allowed on the field even at half time.

10 Similarly, players are not allowed to leave the playing enclosure without the referee's permission.

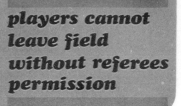

players cannot leave field without referees permission

11 A maximum period of two minutes is permitted for treatment of an injured player. At the end of two minutes the referee should order the injured man's removal unless his removal would be dangerous. After his removal play resumes. He can return to the game only with the referee's permission, and when there is a stoppage of play.

12 It is essential that the referee exercises his authority on behalf of the players. For instance, blowing the whistle harder for a penalty than for a scrum will assist them.

13 His personality is expressed in guidance and friendship to the players, while remaining firm and tactful, consistent in his decisions and clear in his signals. He should not be abusive, aggressive or demonstrative.

14 The referee must carry a whistle and blow it to indicate the beginning of the match, half-time, resumption of play after half-time, off-side, a score or a touch-down.

15 and to stop play because of infringement, or otherwise as required by the laws.

16 He does *not* use his whistle for such purposes as scaring 'a flock of birds from the field of play or to signal to a "bird" in the grandstand.

17 In short, the good referee is one who can get maximum enjoyment for the players and himself, controlling matters from the very beginning so that the players know exactly what he expects of them, and securing their co-operation. He is there to *help* the players, not to domineer them. A pleasant, quiet, but firm manner helps tremendously.

18 The two touch judges are under the control of the referee who may instruct them in their duties and overrule any of their decisions.

19 Rugby law says that the touch judge is there to assist the referee by holding up a flag as soon as the ball (or player carrying it) has gone into touch or touch-in-goal.

20 To do this, he should know when the ball or the player carrying it is in touch. This occurs

21 when the ball, not in a player's possession, touches or crosses the touch line;

22 when a player carrying the ball touches the line or the ground beyond it;

23 or when the ball in the air crosses the touch line, then swerves, or is blown back, into the field of play. It is in touch where it first crosses the line.

24 A player may be in touch, yet play the ball with his foot provided the *ball* is not in touch.

25 And a player in touch or touch-in-goal may score a try, provided he is not carrying the ball. For example, he may be in touch in a corner and dive, from an on-side position, on a rolling ball. He would then score a try.

26 A touch judge raises his flag immediately he decides the ball or the player carrying it has gone into touch, no matter how far away he may be from that point.

27 From that moment he keeps his flag aloft, and subsequently indicates clearly with his free arm which side is entitled to throw in the ball.

28 He lowers the flag smartly as the ball is thrown in, unless the player throwing in the ball puts any part of either foot in the field-of-play,

29 or if the ball is thrown in by the team not entitled to do so. The touch judge is not entitled to keep his flag raised merely because the ball is thrown in from the wrong place.

30 The referee will consult the touch judge after the next dead ball to learn why he kept his flag raised. When told the reasons, he orders the ball to be thrown in again at the site of the line-out where the offence occurred. But this is subject to the advantage law. The referee is always entitled to overrule the touch judge.

31 The touch judge remains *in touch* and is not permitted to go dashing on to the field-of-play to report infringements.

32 Touch judges, are permitted – indeed obliged – to leave the touch-line for kicks at goal following a try or the award of a penalty or free kick. On these occasions the two touch judges stand at or behind the goal posts to signal to the referee whether or not a **goal** has been scored.

33 If he is asked, the touch judge's other function is to help the referee keep time. It is wise, therefore, for the referee and touch judges to synchronise their watches.

34 Remember, the touch judges are under the referee's control and if either touch judge is guilty of misconduct the referee may caution him or even send him from the playing enclosure.

35   Touch judges, obviously, are absolutely impartial and avoid barracking or other evidence of bias.

Questionnaire Part 8

1.   How is a try scored and how many points are awarded?

2.   How is a try converted and what further points are awarded for a successful conversion?

3.   How many points are awarded for a free kick, a penalty kick or a dropped kick?

4.   What is the maximum period permitted for treatment of an injured player on the field?

5.   What are the reasons for the referee to blow his whistle?

6.   What are the functions of the touch judges?

7.   When is a ball in touch?

8.   What are the circumstances that enable a player who is in touch or touch-in-goal to score a try?

9.   What procedure does the touch judge follow from when the ball goes into touch to the throw in?

10.   When is the only time the touch judge may leave the touch-line?

Part 9

Obstruction-Foul Play-Misconduct

1 The original laws of Rugby stated, with remarkable ambiguity, "foul play is illegal". They failed to specify any act as foul play, thus apparently condoning practices that amounted almost to mayhem.

2 One technique then freely in use was the delicate art of hacking. The Rugby Union finally declared this type of violence to be dangerous, and outlawed it. From this beginning the authorities realised that the more vigorous and violent the game became the more rigidly specific the laws had to be made for the safety and enjoyment of players.

3 The laws have been continuously revised to prevent not only foul play and misconduct but also such illegallities as obstruction. Let us consider some specific types of obstruction which the laws forbid.

4 Opposing players running for the ball do not push or hold each other. They may take the shortest distance to the ball and it is quite legal for them to shoulder contact when approaching it.

5 No player may tackle or hold an opponent who is not in possession of the ball. The scrummage is an exception to this but remember, a scrummage ends when the ball comes out.

6 No player may protect a team-mate in possession of the ball. Indeed, a player may never do anything to prevent an opponent tackling the man with the ball.

7 Similarly, an obstruction may occur when a ball carrier runs behind a team-mate, shielding himself from an intended tackle.

8 What is generally known as a *late tackle* is a particularly common and bad form of obstruction. Referees are directed to punish this severely.

9 It is illegal to charge or *in any way obstruct* a player who has just kicked the ball. Often the offender pretends that he started his tackle or charge before his opponent kicked, and could not stop himself. Yet it is amazing how a caution and a penalty kick prevent this alleged accident from occurring again.

10 The early tackle, made before a player receives the ball, is another common form of obstruction, especially after an up and under kick.

•11 For all forms of deliberate obstruction the referee *cautions* the offender, telling him that he will order him from the field if he repeats the offence. After administering the caution he awards a penalty kick to the opposing side at the appropriate place.

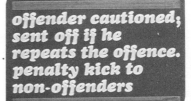

offender cautioned; sent off if he repeats the offence. penalty kick to non-offenders

•12 For a late tackle of a player who has kicked the ball the referee awards a penalty kick at the point of the offence, or where the ball lands or is caught.

13 If the ball alights in touch the penalty is awarded 15 yards infield from where it crossed the touch-line and parallel with the goal line, or at the place where the infringement occurred. The crosses indicate the alternative sites where the penalty may be awarded.

14 If the ball alights within 15 yards of touch, the alternative penalty position is 15 yards infield, parallel with the goal line.

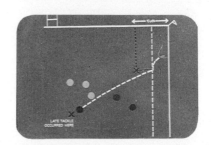

15 If the ball alights over the touch-in-goal line, the penalty is awarded 15 yards in from touch, and five yards from the goal line.

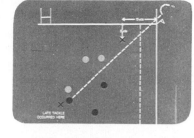

16 If the ball alights within 15 yards of the corner post, the kick may be given 15 yards in from touch and five yards from the goal line, again parallel to the touch line.

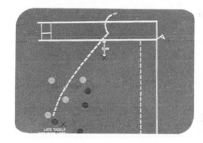

17 If the ball alights in in-goal, or over or on the dead-ball line, the penalty kick is awarded 5 yards from the goal line (on a line parallel to the touch-line) through the place where it crossed the goal line, or 15 yards from the touch-line, whichever gives the greater advantage to the non-offending team.

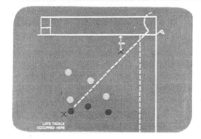

18 But bear in mind that the kick may be taken where the obstruction occurred – which may be in front of the goal posts.

19 Let us now deal with scrummage obstructions. A player may get down, packing widely, providing his binding is legal, but it is illegal for a flanker, or any other player, *to move outwards* from the scrummage, thus preventing a half-back or other opponent from advancing to get the ball.

20   When the ball has emerged from a scrummage it is illegal for a player to continue to hold or bind with an opponent to prevent him from breaking away. Jersey pulling is often the cause of the trouble.

21   It is not illegal to drag away a player lying close to the ball, although this is not allowed in a scrummage or ruck.

22   Line-out obstructions,

23   Lifting,

24   Binding with anyone *while the ball is in the air*,

25 Pushing into anyone *while the ball is in the air,*

26 Barging or shouldering,

27 Protecting half-back by obstruction. You are not allowed to hold a player in the line-out unless he has the ball.

28 Another offence in the line-out is the wedge. Black's number 5 line-out man has caught the ball. His team-mates (at numbers 4 and 6) move in front of him to shield him from their opponents. Numbers 4 and 6 have also put themselves off-side, as well as causing obstruction. They should not be allowed to get away with it.

29 A common felony is the deliberate screen, by players holding out their arms or elbows or packing tightly together while their half-back receives the ball. They should be penalised at once.

30 For all line-out obstructions the referee awards a penalty 15 yards infield on the line-of-touch. But always watch out for an advantage to the non-offending side. Do not be too quick with the whistle, especially when play is near the offender's goal line.

31 The laws forbid any player to molest, obstruct or in any way interfere with an opponent, or be guilty of any form of misconduct while the ball is out of play. Common examples of such offences are

32 kicking or throwing away the ball when the opposition has been awarded a penalty kick;

33 before a line-out;

34 or a scrum;

35   obstructions and other foul play in goal;

36   preventing a defending player from dropping out quickly;

37   and verbal misconduct by any player against an opponent or the referee.

38   For all such offences the referee awards a penalty kick at the place where the ball would have been brought into play if the infringement had not occurred.

39   If the ball is in touch at the time of the infringement, the penalty is awarded on a line at right angles to the touch line, and 10 yards infield from where the ball would have been thrown in.

40 If the infringement occurs in-goal (when the ball is dead) the penalty is awarded at the point where the ball would have been brought into play.

41 It should be unnecessary to remind Rugby players that striking, hacking or kicking an opponent is illegal.

42 Tripping with the foot is illegal, but ankle tapping with the hand is perfectly all right.·

43 This is a stiff arm tackle which must be dealt with immediately and strictly.

44 The laws require a referee to caution or order from the playing enclosure any player or players guilty of foul play or misconduct. A cautioned player committing a similar offence *must* be ordered off. The player should be warned that the laws do not allow a second caution – next time he goes.

45 A referee may issue a general warning to either or both teams for repeated infringements. Any player guilty of misconduct or foul play after such a warning is ordered from the playing enclosure. It is advisable for the referee to call in both captains to support his general warning.

46 If, in his opinion, unfair play or unlawful interference probably prevented the scoring of a try, the referee awards a penalty try – between the goal posts.

47 It is particularly important that the referee's manner does not aggravate players of either side. He remains cool, even when tempers are heated.

48 A halt in play while the referee talks quietly to the players in a general way will often help.

Questionnaire Part 9

1. With the exception of the scrummage, when may a player be tackled?

2. What is a late tackle and how should the referee treat it?

3.   What are the alternative positions for taking a penalty kick, when the ball has gone into touch after an illegality?

4.   What are the alternative positions for taking a penalty kick when the ball has gone into in-goal or over on the dead-ball line after an illegality?

5.   What are some of the common obstructions that occur in a scrummage?

6.   What are some common obstructions in the line-out?

7.   Where will a penalty kick be taken after a line-out penalty?

8.   What forms of misconduct must the referee be watching for while the ball is out of play?

9.   What actions are illegal when tackling a player?

10.   If the referee feels that unfair play or unlawful interference prevented a try being scored what action will he take?

Part 10

Free Kick - Penalty Kick

1 A drop-*out* is a drop kick by the defending team after a touch-down, or after the ball has touched or crossed the touch-in-goal or dead ball lines having been last played by an attacking player.

2 A drop-*kick* is made by a player dropping the ball from his hands to the ground and kicking it on its first rebound. A drop-*out* is taken anywhere on or behind the defending side's 25 yard line. If the kick is not taken within this area the referee orders the drop-out to be taken again.

3 If the drop-out does not carry the ball as far as the kicking side's 25 yard line, the opposing side may have it dropped out again, or have a set scrum on the centre of the 25 yard line. This applies even if the wind prevents the ball from reaching the line, if it reaches the line and is blown back, play continues, subject to the advantage law.

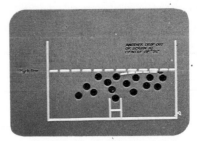

4 If any of the kicker's team are in front of the ball when it is dropped out, the referee orders a scrum on the centre of the 25 yard line.

5   If the opposing team charges over the 25 yard line, the ball must be dropped out again.

6   If the ball pitches in touch from a drop-out, the opposing team has the choice of a scrum in the centre of the 25 yard line, another drop-out, or a line-out where the ball crossed the touch-line.

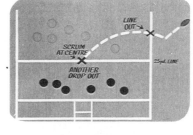

7   A quick drop-out is quite legal, provided that the ball is drop-kicked from within the 25, the ball crosses the 25 yard line, and all players of the kicker's team are behind the ball when it is kicked.

8   Players of the non-kicking side do not have to be outside their opponents' 25 yard line at the time of the drop-out; but the referee should deal promptly with any player obstructing or attempting to obstruct a quick drop-out.

9   Many Rugby spectators and players wrongly refer to a penalty kick as a free kick. A *free-kick* is one allowed for a fair catch, and may be taken as a place kick, drop-kick, or punt.

10 The free-kick is taken at or behind the mark where the fair catch was made. The opposing team may come up to, but not beyond, a line passing through the mark, parallel with the goal lines.

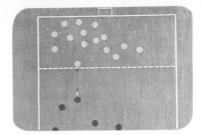

11 They may charge the player taking a drop-kick or punt as soon as he begins his run, or in any way offers to kick.

12 If the marker elects to place-kick, the opposition may charge as soon as the ball touches the ground. The kicker should use a team-mate to hold and place the ball.

13 If the opposing players fairly charge and prevent the kick from being taken, the referee orders a set scrum, *on the mark,* with the charging side to put in the ball.

14 A ball knocked forward (even from the hand or arm) in a charge-down, is not treated as a knock-on unless the player attempts to catch the ball.

15 If the opposition charges unfairly (that is before the kicker begins his run or shapes to kick), then the kicker is awarded a free kick, which opponents are not allowed to charge.

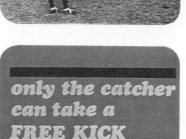

16 The player making the fair catch and calling "Mark!", is the *only* one who may take the free kick. If he is injured and cannot recover sufficiently to take it within two minutes, the free kick is forfeited and a scrummage is set on the mark.

only the catcher can take a FREE KICK

•17 The ball goes forward and should reach a line through the mark, which is also parallel with the goal lines, unless first played by an opponent. It does not necessarily have to pass *through* the mark.

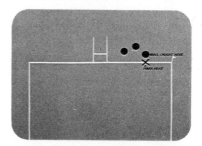

18 If the fair catch is in-goal, the mark is on the goal line opposite where the ball is caught. The opposition may charge, as elsewhere in the field. If any of the catcher's team-mates infringes after a fair catch in-goal, the referee orders a scrum five yards from the goal-line and opposite the mark.

19 A ball kicked from a fair catch "in-goal" must cross the goal line, unless first played by an opponent. If first played by the kicker's team, or if the opposing team lawfully prevents the kick from being taken, a five yards scrum is awarded.

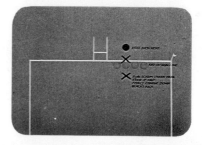

20 The referee awards a penalty kick against a team infringing the laws. The kicker may punt, drop-kick or place-kick the ball. He may score a penalty goal from either a drop- or place-kick. The non-offending team is not forced to accept a penalty kick but may take a scrummage instead.

21 The place at which the referee awards the penalty is on a line through the mark and parallel to the touch-lines. If the place is within five yards of the offending team's goal-line, the mark is five yards from their goal-line; this also applies if a scrummage is taken.

mark for penalty kick must not be within five yards of offenders goal line

22 From a penalty, the ball may be kicked in any direction and it need not travel any specified distance. After it has been kicked *anyone,* including the kicker, may play it. But the ball must have been kicked, that is, propelled by the foot or leg. A tap kick is perfectly legal because the ball has been propelled, even through only a few inches.

23 This is not a kick. The kicker has touched the ball with his foot, but he has not released it from his hands so the ball has not been propelled.

24 Having indicated to the referee by word or action that he intends to try for goal from a penalty kick, the kicker must do so.

25 He may not go through the motions of preparing to kick at goal, then suddenly play a tap kick or an up and under.

26 For any infringement by the kicker's team following a penalty kick, the referee orders a scrummage on the mark, with the opposition putting in the ball.

27 There is benefit to be had from careful study of the laws governing the award of a penalty.

Questionnaire Part 10

1. What is a drop-out?

2. What is a drop-kick?

3. Where may a drop-out be taken and what happens if the ball does not reach the kicking side's 25 yard line?

4. What choices does the opposing team have if the ball from a drop-out pitches in touch?

5. When is a free-kick allowed and how is it taken?

6. If the player making the fair catch and calling "Mark" is injured and unable to take the free-kick within two minutes, what decision does the referee take?

7.   When is a penalty kick awarded and what alternative may the non-offending team take?

8.   If an infringement takes place within five yards of the offending team's goal-line, where will the penalty kick be taken?

9.   In which direction can a penalty kick be made and who may play it immediately after it has been kicked?

10.   What decision will the referee give for an infringement by the kicker's team following a penalty kick?

Part 11

Penalty Kick - The Try

1 Probably the most effective deterrent to illegal play in Rugby is the penalty kick. We have seen some of the advantages the award of a penalty bestows on the non-offending side. Now let us see what obligations it imposes on the offenders.

2 They retire without delay to an imaginary line parallel to their goal line and 10 yards on their side of the mark. The kicker need not delay his kick until all his opponents have gone back 10 yards.

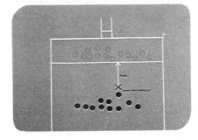

3 The opponents are required to run these **10** yards, and to do nothing else (even while the ball is being played) until they have. A quickly taken penalty kick often catches a number of opponents temporarily *out of the game.*

4 When a penalty is awarded within 10 yards of the offender's goal line, they need retire only as far as this goal line – but they must remain there until the kick is taken.

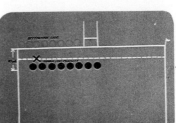

5 Except when a quick tap kick is taken from a penalty, the opponents usually have time to retire the required distance. Having got there, they remain passive and motionless with their hands by their sides until the ball has been kicked. This is particularly important when a kick at goal is being taken.

6 When the kick is taken very quickly, it is sometimes impossible for *all* the penalised side's players to get 10 yards back from the mark. But they must continue to run in that direction, not interferring with play or stopping to await results, *unless a player of the kicker's team has run five yards carrying the ball.*

7 If any of the offending team infringe any of these laws, the referee awards *another* penalty against them, this time 10 yards closer to their own goal line, through the original mark. The referee may award a succession of such penalties for sluggish retirement or interference with the kicker's team.

8 Referees do not penalise players genuinely trying (but unable) to retire 10 yards before the ball is kicked. Note that passing or kicking the ball does not automatically put these players on-side.

9 An attacking player scores a try by being the first to ground the ball, after *carrying* it to the opponent's in-goal;

after it has been kicked into the in-goal

11   or after a scrummage has been pushed over the goal line. Scrummage laws, such as handling the ball and binding, do not apply because, when the ball is over the goal line, it is no longer in the scrum. A scrummage can take place only in the field of play.

12   Also, when the ball is over the line, any player may break from the scrum *and* get in front of the ball.

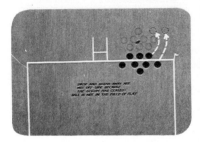

13   A player may score a try even though his feet are in touch or touch-in-goal provided he is not carrying the ball. And remember, the corner post is touch-in-goal. Here we see a player diving on a loose ball while his feet are in touch-in-goal. This is a try.

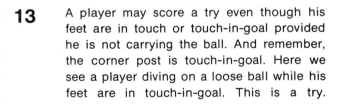

14   The goal-lines are in-goal. A try is scored if the ball is grounded on the goal-line. And, since the goal-posts are part of the goal line, a ball properly grounded against a post scores a try.

15 Grounding the ball means bringing it in contact with the ground while holding it;

16 or by exerting downward pressure on it with a hand or arm if the ball is already on the ground;

17 or by falling on the ball so that it is under the *front* of the body, from the waist to the neck.

18 Picking up the ball is *not* grounding it. A player picking it up is *not* exerting downward pressure. This fellow may lose the ball before grounding it.

19 A defending player obtains a touch-down by first grounding the ball in his own in-goal. When this happens the referee awards a drop-out.

If the touch-down occurs after a defending player has heeled, kicked, passed, knocked,

21 or carried the ball over his own goal-line, the referee orders a five yard scrummage infield from the point where the ball crossed the line.

22 If a defender kicks or knocks the ball over his own dead ball line or goal line, from the field of play, the referee awards a five yard scrum from the position where the ball was last played by a defender.

23 If the ball touches a defender who makes no attempt to play it before it crosses his own goal-line, and the ball becomes dead, the referee awards a drop-out.

24 But if a defender touches the ball in trying to play is before it crosses his goal-line, and it afterwards becomes dead, the referee awards a five yard scrummage from the position where the ball was intentionally touched.

25   A referee signals his award of a try by blowing his whistle, raising his arm **vertically**, then standing on the goal line in line with the point at which the ball was grounded.

26   The referee may alter his decision if he has failed to notice that a touch-judge's flag was raised, and accepts the touch-judge's opinion that the player went into touch or knocked against the corner post before grounding the ball. He then orders a line-out or a drop-out. But the referee may over-rule the touch-judge.

27   After awarding a try, the referee ensures that a kick at goal is taken along the right line, that all the kicker's team are behind the kicker, and that the opponents are behind their own goal-line.

28   As soon as the kicker begins his run or offers to kick, the opposing players may charge or jump to prevent a goal being scored.

29   But they may not charge prematurely, creep forward beyond the goal line, or otherwise try to distract the kicker. For any such offence, the referee rules "no charge". In these circumstances, if the kick is successful he allows a goal; if not he allows the kicker another attempt, which may not be charged.

30 When the referee cannot decide which side first grounded the ball in goal, he orders a five yard scrummage opposite this point. The attacking side puts in the ball.

31 The referee will also order a five yard scrum when a player in-goal is so held that he cannot ground the ball. Again the attacking side will put the ball into the scrum.

32 You see, the emphasis is always on ATTACK.

Questionnaire Part 11

1. When a penalty kick is to be taken where must the offending team place themselves?

2. If a penalty is awarded within ten yards of the offender's goal line, where must the offending team place themselves?

3. If a penalty kick is taken very quickly and the offending team are not ten yards back, what must they do?

4. If any of the offending team commit an infringement during the taking of a penalty, what decision will the referee make?

5. How is a try scored?

6.   If a player has his feet in touch or touch-in-goal, how may he score a try?

7.   What decision will be given if the ball is grounded on the goal posts?

8.   What is meant by grounding the ball?

9.   What happens if a defending player obtains a touch-down first in his own in-goal?

10.   At what stage may the opposing team charge, when a kick at goal is being taken?